Restoring What Was Lost

Expressions of Pain, Love and Renewal

Elanna N. Wells

BookLeaf Publishing

India | USA | UK

Dedication

To my kids, Riveria, Iana and Edwuanis,Jr. they have
always been my motivation to do this.
I always felt I had the gift of writing but always felt I
couldn't accomplish my dreams.
life will always be the greatest teacher, very beautiful
and painful at the same time.
This is also dedicated to a "Friend" .... a Friend who
taught me to never give up, life is not over until it is
over.
just take a moment to live life and just enjoy the
moments.
This Is my moment!!!

Preface

To all the moments that shaped me, The painful situations that made me stronger, and the growth that created who i am today.

Acknowledgements

Fulfilling this dream has been challenging, I am so grateful that I seen it through. I would like to Thank everyone who believed in me and keep encouraging me throughout the years to put my words out there for to help breathe life into someone you will never know who you will touch. Without people believing in me this book would have never come to life.

Pain

I can't wrap my mind around the root of my pain.
distance.....isolation can drive a person insane.
Just please oh, please take away the pain.
I suppress things that negatively feeds my soul
whatever your vice
please think twice
it may add to the tragedy of your endless story
turn the page
close the chapters that rewind you back to that bad mind
frame.
But embrace the pleasures of the pain
pain produce growth
also, pain keeps you woke
makes you feel alive
otherwise, pain can end up being your demise.
pain can also produce an emotion that cannot be
described
and emotion that cannot be defined
only in due time will pain reveal the beauty it can
produce inside.

Where are you?

As I take this Alone time to prepare myself for you
I just don't want to be "a wife"
I want to be "your" wife
I'm preparing myself for you
I want to be mentally and spiritually fit to be exactly
what you need.
Love God and myself,
to love and support you and to be your help meet.
Uncover myself from anger
depression...self-pity
learning to love and build a relationship with God
All the things that block me from you, so that you will
be able to find me.
when a man finds a wife, he finds a good thing and
obtains favor from the lord
So, while I prepare for you,
My Husband
Love God, Pray for me
Cause soon you will be able to see me.

The Monarchy

A king and a queen sit on the throne
the queen does not sit beneath him
She sits beside him.... her presence is what makes him
great...
her strength ...her dignity makes him stand tall.
She encourages him...she keeps him focused.
In return...
He honors...respects and loves her...no one
can disrespect his queen...not even him.
He admires her strength...he relishes in her virtue
respects her mind...her body and soul
The two can be a force to be reckoned with
no one could come between the empire they will build
I'm preparing myself for my king
so, I can be all he needs and desires
and I can bring life into his soul.
Without you king, there is know me.
I watch over you and cover you in prayer.
no one can match what we share
our mere existence is because I breathe the same air as

you breathe.
the way our love with stand will always remain a
mystery
told by folk lore and passed down in history.
our love displayed on a blank canvas
for people to see our happiness for centuries to come
My king, you are my world
I am your queen, my reason for being.

My Plea

I'm in this mode
because i never felt protected
I always provided my blanket and pillow for my safety.
It's my place of solitude
Very quiet
nothing but peace
in my thoughts, in these walls
I've created
my own sense of security
False sense of hope because i always had it rough
I've gotten to a place
where i want to be so at peace
that i can only hear God speak to me
I want to feel that every moment, every second
is filled with his presence
I want to scream so loudly
DONT GIVE UP ON ME!!! YET
My heart is yearning
for you to touch my soul
Forgiveness will be spoken so proudly

i want to clean my soul of negativity
I want to get myself right.
I want all my desires to come when i am ready
Lord i just want to lay in your hands
and get ready for the blessings you have before me
Change me lord
I don't want to hurt anymore and lash out at anyone
with the pain of my past ...
i dont want to be bound to anyone that is still connected
to anything or anyone toxic
cleanse me
heal me ....i dont want to remain the same.
In your mighty name
Amen.....

I will

That day will come when my skin will be flawless
my hair will be strong
my walk will have a bounce to it
my presence will be felt without any words being spoken
When I speak, I will have the confidence like no other
I will
be at peace
no longer worry about who's going to love me
cause my love for me will surpass any love that i thought
i never had.
My smile will brighten up a room
strangers will love me and don't have no idea why
It's my ora
My inner peace will shine bright like a diamond.
I will be fearless
i will overcome any pain and traumas
hat have taken over me for years
i will walk alone and i will still have happiness
Waiting on my king
in the mist of my journey

when i am found
everything that i am i will multiply
u see i will be his peace
cause i was peaceful before him
I will be home to him
because i already know how to make a house a home
I will be his place of rest
because my soul will already be ready to submit
My feminine energy will now be at an all-time high
Because i have finally meet him
he found me...he found love
his good thing in a world of chaos
he is amazed that i still exist
in a world that thrives off of who i can love next
I am a wife
and i will carry myself in that manner
one day i will be ruth and he will be my boaz.
I will.....take care of me
Until he is ready to provide the space for me to be "his
woman"
I will be like a little girl again
knowing I am loved and protected
i want to have to be strong anymore
i want to have to fight for love anymore
i don't want a temporary fix
i want what God has for me
so until then I will Wait.......

Sunday Morning

He reminds me of Sunday mornings,
the peace of the air,
the rays of the sun hitting the windowpane.
He reminds me that not all me are the same.
My Sunday Morning,
Where i feel safe in his arms,
mesmerized by his smell,
Hypnotized by his words when he speaks,
feeling his heartbeat as he lays next to me.
His presence brings me comfort
his laugh brings me joy.
My Sunday Morning
is the one moment where time stands still and i rejoice.
The day of rest, the day of reflection
that is him
He is my blessing.

Thats me

They say I'm conservative
So, that's my style
They say I'm traditional
Well, tradition brings me smiles
They think I'm old fashioned
but it just isn't so,
They think I'm an angel
But what do they know?

Enchanted evening

I'm not here to complain
I'm here to comply
if you are ready to be mine
I can explain why
Cause I'm ready to pour into you and watch your love
overflow
I have a strong belief
U are not ready for me
I hear your heartbeat race
when I'm lying on your chest
Your breathing becomes slower
as you try to speak
I make your knees weak
U just don't want to admit that I can make you submit
I kiss you
u moan
I ride you
you say my name
I want to hear you say it again
So, I slow up the rhythm right before you climax,

Let me teach you about me
because you never explored this
type of love before
I'm a spiritual goddess
with levels of pleasure
and I guarantee you
No one before me will ever measure
My name holds weight
Ms. Neffy soul is spritually enchanted.

Tranquility

I'm so ready
Not to be strong
not to be afraid to submit
finally have a place to belong.
My feminine energy
is ready to emerge
from being in the mode of playing the role
of mother and father
remind me that I'm a woman
in the space you have provided
a space for us to pray and love one another.
I love you too much
I would have to be out of love with you for me to let
someone else in.
I love you too much not to risk losing you
just to gain a little of attention,
I'm right in the place I need to be
a place of love, A place of serenity.
A place called tranquility.

a life never defined

a seed, conceived
already determined
to rest in peace
never will be able to
see mom and dad's face,
My child is already in his final resting place.
a lost loved one
that has never left my memory
because the connection we shared
could never be erased.
detached from my womb but never my heart
I was your mother but, God knew my plans from the
start
Instead of my love flowing through your veins
it flows through my words
my dear child
hold on for a while
maybe God will reincarnate
you into my grandchild.
one day I will see you again

my bundle of pride and joy.
Our souls will rejoice
I am your mother; I won't be hard to find.
I'm so sorry
I didn't give you a chance to have your life defined.

.

In just 30 seconds

Slowly I'm dying
I've injected something into my soul
that can erase me from all humanity
Killing what is left of me
I look at myself in the mirror
trying to recapture what I've lost
I'm willing to regain my soul at any cost.
Self-justification
lead me to the door of instant gratification
all of this to sooth my battered ego
i need that constant rush
It felt better than a man's touch
this shit had me in a world of lust
The only thing i could trust...
The deadliest sin is corrupting my memory.
Living my life in one scene
Chasing after unrealistic dreams
Shit, I'm tired of singing the same ole song....
U know what.... Fuck it I'm gone!!

divine purpose

God made a woman a man's help mate
his rib, we were only created and designed for only the
one.
The key to this whole process is "he" has to find you...
but after he finds himself
you are not to be loved by every man u encounter, not
every man will uphold you up to high regards
not every man sees you or sees how good you are
your goodness will be seen by the man that will find you
with purpose.
By purpose... I mean his love for you is already there
he will have respect for you
he will provide your needs
so that he can fit in your life where he needs to
his questions won't be what i can get from you
but where do you need me to be.
"woman" you are divinely designed for one man...
until he finds you, you will not fit as his rib
because you are only made for the one "god" divinely
send to you

Love is

Love is Patient
Endures All things
and never loses hope
Loving someone is to love with no conditions
its choosing to love them even though
it's hard to do so.
if you are loving someone and they meet your
expectations
and once they step out of your expectations and you are
done with them
Thats not love.
You are loving them as long as they be what you want.
I'm still waiting on my king to emerge
so that my love can give him everything he deserves
my love is patient
when it's like that no one or nothing can distract you
from it.

Try, and Try Again

Never define a man or woman by the flaws
A flaw is an imperfection of one's weaknesses
Raise your hands if you dont have one
mmmmm....i doubt if anyone will.
But measure a man or a woman on their character
...things that they will do without question
A man can fall so many times
but it takes strength and acknowledge your
shortcomings
and get back up and try again
the only thing worse than trying
is giving up completely.

Her Beauty inside (Just Beautiful)

You are God's greatest treasure.
Blessed beyond measure.
Do you even know the value of you.
God created woman to be the helper of a man
to endure all trials and tribulations
and still smile in the mist of trouble.
Thats why everyday you walk his earth should be a
celebration
She wears may hats
She is the doctor, the lawyer
The peacemaker, she places the world on her shoulders
and carry it like feathers.
you will never know how she truly feels because the
wellbeing of the ones she cares
for is the only thing that matters...
Her love can never be replaced
with her arms placed around you
it is the most peaceful place.
when we love we love hard

Family is our greatest accomplishment
A woman exceeds all expectations but gets little award.
But she doesn't ask for it. God created her as a gift and a
help mate.
to be a man's pride ... she wears many hats and will
never break her stride.
with her head held high... love and protect her...
look at her now...
do I need to give you any more reasons why?

Alluring Thoughts

I need an excuse for my reaction for the way my body
receives you...
it's a natural reaction.
The Flashbacks have become a distraction...
U see my mind is on you daily....
My soul has been craving you lately.
I'm having an orgasmic revelation...
It is combination of love and hate...
with a touch of joy and regret...
When your soul enters mine...
My walls begin to sweat
with each stroke....
You break down the bars that has my heart barricaded...
From my past hurts that cannot be faded........to be
continued.......

No longer

I no longer want to say I'm, ok?
I no longer want to smile to cover up the hurt
I no longer want to be a benefit to others
when it's convenient for them
I will give my last
My testimony will speak for itself
if I could tell my story, it will uncover me
it's not time to tell it when my story isn't done yet.
I no longer want to just love me
I want to be in love with me.
I have to embrace my pain. and forgive those that have
hurt me.
especially the ones that did it unknowingly.
My forgiveness starts with me...
I have to forgive myself for the pain i have caused,
others and myself
because if I had more love for me, nothing or no one
could affect me.
I said all this to acknowledge my growth
I have disconnected myself with others to get

reacquainted with myself
and learn how to reconnect in a better way.

. No one never knew

Cover my mouth from speaking
no one will ever know my soul has been beaten
I have no physical scars, no bruises but on the inside I'm
useless.
I'm your bitch, in the dark corners of our home
I'm in a house full of people but yet i feel so alone.
but, in the light of day, I'm your queen, your wife
Someone you want to be with for the rest of your life,
at night you turn to the other woman
her name Snow white. You loved her with all your might,
She took everything but left your soul,
she made you so mean so cold.
u camouflage the addiction of her,
as time went on the real story starts to
unfold. her demands became too constant and in our
home your presence became more distant.
but I continued to cover my mouth to keep from
speaking
no one and I mean no one will know my soul has been
beaten.

at night, I see the devil in my home with no warning,
I cry out to God... I pray that i can make it until morning.

October 1...

Love created me... Conceived by a husband and a wife.
Born prematurely to the world,
not one seed but two.
first one to the world, I was defined
as a miracle baby, weighing one pound 12 ounces
deemed as the oldest.
Showing signs of improvement, my twin could not
survive
Her purpose was to return to God.
My purpose was to stay in this world and prove my
strength.
My strength was to define all odds ...and leave an
imprint on this world.
I'm more than just me... I am a survivor....

Good morning....beautiful

Hey Beautiful

Are you ok?

It's been a while since we last spoke

it's been a minute since i seen you smile

i am here to remind you

you are going to be alright...

see, the past prepared you for the now.

Your strength made you grow

The pain people inflicted on you did not destroy you.

But guess what

You are still here.

To see another day....

You are amazing... A beautiful soul and that my dear no

one can take from you.

The shift in the room is only there because of your

presence

When you enter a person's life

Blessings Flows through you

That they will be able to feel you even in your absence.

I just want to remind you today of who you are and let

you know you are loved.

keep going, keep striving. Live!!!!!Be above the rest

Love Always,

Your inner self

Crowning Glory

I've been called weird on many occasions.
people saying I think I am better than everyone else
as I get older, I only think twice on my decisions.
I walk alone Because the way the world moves
I feel I just don't belong.
I try to give my assistance
but my presence scares people away from my helping
hands.
My spirit is overwhelming
My grace is undeniable, once I enter into your life
My foot tracks cannot be erased.
I am favored, I am blessed
My skin is so tough, I can handle any test.
I am a vessel, That God speaks Through. God, I don't
understand,
But I have to understand it's all in your plans
to love my fellow neighbor and do unto them as u would
do to me,
I walk this journey because I can handle it.
I treat people how I want to be treated

Nurturing souls back to health even though I deplete
from myself.
in the mist of the storms, I have to cry out why
god said I have to use you, all I can do is sigh
In the end of my walk in this valley
my blessings will overflow, it will be shown to many
No one will ever know that my place at the table was
already prepared
God dwell in the mist of silence
not in a world of chaotic motions
I move the way I move Because of my love for God,
Acknowledge his presence and respect it.
So, if I am weird for following Gods plan
It's not for me to explain and surely not for the world to
understand.